The Christmas Morning Sneak

by
A. H. Walker

illustrated by
John Walker

The Christmas Morning Sneak
Copyright 2014 by A. H. Walker

All rights reserved. Please do not duplicate any portion of this book without the express consent of the author. Remember, Santa is watching.

Published by Piscataqua Press
An imprint of RiverRun Bookstore
142 Fleet St., Portsmouth NH 03801

www.piscataquapress.com

ISBN: 978-1-939739-44-5

Printed in the United States of America

Then there came a loud squeak, and it made us stop dead.

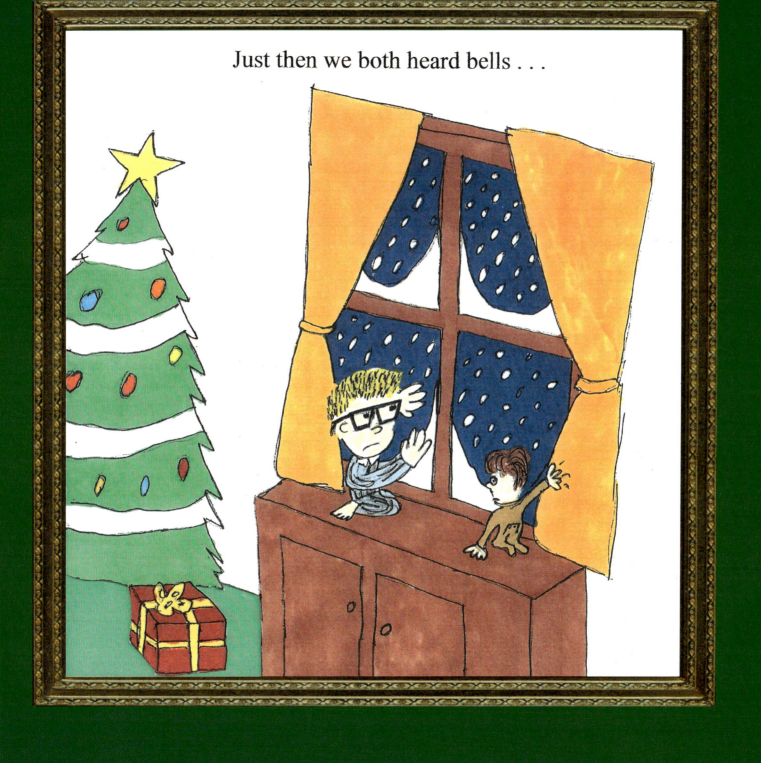

and climbing into bed, fearing that if
Santa had seen us awake, and not asleep

All our presents in his big sack, he would just keep.

and tip-toeing down, hoping there was something to be found.

Yes! There were presents piled up under that tree.

And one great big one left just for me!

The origin of the story, *The Christmas Morning Sneak*

I wrote this story in poem form about a memory of my little brother and me trying to sneak downstairs and see Santa Claus early on Christmas morning. The story takes place in 1959, when I, (Big Al) was eight years old, and Tommy, (a.ka. Tinky Tom) was only four years old.

Upon completion of the poem, I gave copies to the teachers where I work as Christmas presents. They, in turn, read the poem to classes of high school students who they reported enjoyed it immensely. Apparently it brought back fond memories of their own childhood. Many people began to tell me they thought it would make a great children's book.

Agreeing with their idea, I enlisted the talents of my 34 year old autistic son, John, who is an accomplished artist. This project became a father-son collaboration that I am extremely proud of. Although the process was long, and sometimes tedious, it turned into a heartfelt bonding experience between John and myself.

Being an artist, I was surprised to learn more from John that I ever thought possible. He certainly exceeded my expectations! John's visual perception of the story solidified the emotions my brother and I felt that day so long ago.

About the Author

Al Walker enjoys writing poetry and has co-authored with his wife, a memoir of his son, who lives with autism. *The Christmas Morning Sneak* is the first children's book he has written although he has plans for more in the works. Al has published some of his poems in periodicals and continues to write poetry.

He is an artist, as well, and loves to paint and draw. Another hobby he enjoys is working with wood. Al hopes to have more time for these hobbies when he retires soon.

Al grew up in Portsmouth and has lived there his entire life. He studied art and writing in the Portsmouth school system. Al enjoys living in New England and is interested in this region's history.

About the Illustrator

John Walker, a 34 year-old man living with autism, is the subject of his parents' memoir, *Bringing Up John: One Family's Life with Autism.* He has been drawing since early childhood and loves creating cartoon characters. He currently works with a local cartoonist, Chet Buckley, helping him with his comic books.

John also enjoys painting during his art class and has exhibited his works at two art shows organized by his instructor, Darlene Furbush Ouellett. He continues to hone his skills by drawing, painting, and also writing nearly every day of his life.

John has a love for all forms of art and music and considers autism a gift, not a disability. He understands that it allows him to see the world through an enhanced prism, which contributes greatly to his creativity.

CPSIA information can be obtained
at www.ICGtesting.com
Printed in the USA
BVXC01n1228231014
371617BV00003B/6